Accounting for Leases

Steven M. Bragg

AccountingTools®

Table of Contents

About the Author

Steven Bragg, CPA, has been the chief financial officer or controller of four companies, as well as a consulting manager at Ernst & Young. He received a master's degree in finance from Bentley College, an MBA from Babson College, and a Bachelor's degree in Economics from the University of Maine. He has been a two-time president of the Colorado Mountain Club, and is an avid alpine skier, mountain biker, and certified master diver. Mr. Bragg resides in Centennial, Colorado. He has written more than 300 books and courses, including *New Controller Guidebook*, *GAAP Guidebook*, and *Payroll Management*. He has also written *The Auditors* science fiction trilogy.

Steven maintains the accountingtools.com web site, which contains continuing professional education courses, the Accounting Best Practices podcast, and thousands of articles on accounting subjects.

Buy Additional AccountingTools Courses

AccountingTools offers more than 1,500 hours of CPE courses, with concentrations in accounting, auditing, finance, taxation, and ethics. Related courses that you might like include:

- Accountants' Guidebook
- Corporate Finance

Go to accountingtools.com/cpe to view these additional courses.

AccountingTools

Accounting for Leases

Introduction

This course addresses the core concepts surrounding the accounting for leases by all parties entering into these arrangements. There are several fundamental leasing issues that we will cover in the following pages, including the following:

- *Types of leases*. There are several possible designations that can be applied to a lease, depending upon the facts and circumstances associated with it. Each of these designations triggers a different set of accounting rules.
- *Balance sheet recognition*. One of the key aspects of the accounting for leases is that lease assets and lease liabilities are now recognized on the balance sheet. Under previous guidance, it was possible for lessees to keep certain leases off their balance sheets, which masked their true financial condition.
- *Elections*. There are several lease-related elections that an entity can take, which are generally designed to simplify the accounting for leases.
- *Disclosures*. The presentation and disclosure rules for leases are quite extensive, in order to provide the maximum amount of information to the readers of an organization's financial statements.

The accounting rules discussed in this course are derived from the Accounting Standards Codification (ASC) 842, *Leases*, which replace the rules previously categorized under ASC 840, *Leases*. The key difference between these two standards is that most leases must now be capitalized on the balance sheet of the lessee. The change was made to counteract the tendency of many companies to structure their leases to keep lease-related assets and liabilities off their balance sheets.

The Nature of a Lease

A lease is an arrangement under which a lessor agrees to allow a lessee to control the use of identified property, plant, and equipment for a stated period of time in exchange for one or more payments. A lease arrangement is quite a useful opportunity, for the following reasons:

- The lessee reduces its exposure to asset ownership
- The lessee obtains financing from the lessor in order to pay for the asset
- The lessee now has access to the leased asset

An arrangement is considered to give control over the use of an asset when both of these conditions are present:

- The lessee obtains the right to substantially all of the economic benefits from using an asset; and
- The lessee obtains the right to direct the uses to which an asset is put.

EXAMPLE

Blitz Communications obtains the rights to the entire output of an undersea cable for the next ten years, in order to benefit from an expected increase in traffic from new data centers in Sweden to users in the United States. Since Blitz has the right to substantially all of the economic benefits from using the cable, the underlying contract is considered a lease. If the arrangement had instead been for only a certain proportion of the total capacity of the cable, where the cable operator could choose which fibers within the cable would carry Blitz's data, the arrangement would not be considered a lease.

EXAMPLE

The Cupertino Beanery enters into a contract to operate a store from retail space. Part of the contract states that Cupertino must pay 10% of its revenues to the landlord. Cupertino still obtains the right to substantially all of the economic benefits from using the retail space – subsequent to obtaining the revenues, the company then pays 10% to the landlord. This contract clause does not prevent the contract from being designated as a lease.

EXAMPLE

Teton Helicopter Rescue leases a helicopter for use in its personnel rescue operations. As part of the lease agreement, Teton is only allowed to operate the helicopter during daylight hours. This restriction is designed to reduce the risk of damage to the craft. This protective right limits the scope of Teton's usage of the helicopter, but does not actually prevent it from having the right to use the asset. Thus, the restriction does not prevent the contract from being designated as a lease.

The following additional points all apply to whether a lease exists:

- *Partial period*. If a leasing arrangement only lasts for a portion of the period spanned by a contract, a lease is still presumed to exist for the partial period specified within the contract.
- *Right of substitution*. If a contract allows the supplier to substitute an identified asset with another asset throughout the usage period, there is no lease. This situation only applies when the supplier has the practical ability to substitute alternative assets, and the supplier obtains a positive economic benefit from doing so. The evaluation of the ability to substitute assets does not include assets that are unlikely to occur.

EXAMPLE

Nautilus Tours leases several submarines from Underwater Assets, for use in shallow-water tourist visits to nearby reefs. The lease agreement states that Underwater Assets can substitute a submarine for repairs or maintenance in the event that a submarine is not operating properly. This contract language still allows Nautilus Tours to have the right to an identified asset, so the existence of the lease is not called into question.

EXAMPLE

Nova Corporation operates a deep field scanning telescope for sky survey work, which it leases from Alpha Centauri Leasing. If the contract language is interpreted in a certain way, it appears possible that Alpha could substitute the telescope at a later date. However, the telescope is located at Nova's observatory, and would be difficult to dismount and replace. The cost of substitution is therefore likely to be higher than any benefits that Alpha might gain from the substitution. In this case, it appears likely that there is a lease.

EXAMPLE

Grissom Granaries stores corn and wheat along the Mississippi River. It enters into an agreement with a local transport firm to transport crops up and down the river. The volume of transport services indicated in the contract translates into the ongoing use of 10 barges. The transport firm has several hundred barges that it can use to fulfill the contract. When not in use, the barges are stored at one of the transport firm's riverside facilities. No specific barges are described in the contract. Given these conditions, it is apparent that Grissom does not direct the use of the barges, nor does it have the right to obtain substantially all of the economic benefits from use of the barges. Consequently, this arrangement is not a lease.

EXAMPLE

The Hegemony Toy Company enters into a contract with an international shipping company to deliver a shipload of goods from Singapore to Los Angeles. The specific freighter to be used is named in the contract, and only Hegemony's board games will be shipped. However, the shipping company will operate the freighter during the voyage. This arrangement is not a lease, since Hegemony cannot direct the uses to which the freighter is put.

Since the accounting for a lease only applies to property, plant, and equipment, it does not apply to the following types of assets that may also be leased:

- Assets under construction
- Biological assets (such as orchards)
- Exploration assets (such as oil and gas exploration rights)
- Intangible assets
- Inventory

> **Tip:** As will become apparent throughout this course, the lease accounting requirements are burdensome. To keep from designating an arrangement as a lease, insert into the underlying contract a statement that the lessor has the right to substitute the asset being leased with another asset of equivalent or greater value at any time. This language prevents the arrangement from being designated as a lease; instead, it is a service contract, for which the accounting is greatly simplified.

Lease Components (Lessee)

Once it has been established that a contract contains a lease, it is necessary to separate the lease into its components (if any). This can result in a business tracking several different leases within one contract. A separate lease component exists when both of the following conditions are present:

- The lessee can benefit from the right of use of a single asset, or together with other readily available resources; and
- The right of use is separate from the rights to use other assets in the contract. This is not the case when the rights of use of the different assets significantly affect each other.

The right to use land is always considered a separate lease component, unless doing so would have an insignificant effect.

EXAMPLE

Treetops Telecommunications leases a cell phone tower, along with the land on which it is positioned and the building within which it is located. The building was designed specifically to house the cell phone tower and related equipment. In this case, the rights of use of the different assets significantly affect each other, so one lease arrangement encompasses all of the assets. The inclusion of the land component in the same lease is considered to have an insignificant effect.

There may also be non-lease components to a contract. These components will not meet the criteria just stated for a lease component, but will transfer a good or service to the lessee. There may also be other activities that do not qualify as non-lease components, since there is no transfer of goods or services; for example, the reimbursement of lessor costs falls into this category.

A common charge associated with a lease is common area maintenance. The lessor typically performs maintenance and cleaning services for all common areas in a building, and then charges a portion of these costs through to the building tenants. The lessee would otherwise have to perform these services itself or pay a third party to do so. Common area maintenance costs are considered a non-lease component.

The classifications of lease components are not reassessed after the commencement date of the lease, unless the contract is subsequently modified and the change is not treated as a separate contract. Lease classifications can also be revisited if the lease term changes or there is a change in the probability that an option will be exercised to purchase an underlying asset.

Once all lease and non-lease components have been identified, allocate the consideration in the contract to them. This allocation is derived as follows:

1. Determine the standalone price of each separate lease and non-lease component. This should be based on the observable standalone price. If this price is not available, it can be estimated.
2. Allocate the consideration in proportion to the standalone prices of the various components.
3. If there are any initial direct costs associated with the contract, allocate these costs on the same basis as the lease payments.

EXAMPLE

Micron Metallic leases a stamping machine and a CNC (computer numerical control) machine for its washing machine production facility, along with periodic maintenance and repair services. The total consideration that Micron will pay over the five-year term of the lease is $800,000.

Micron's controller concludes that there are two separate leases, since the stamping and CNC machines are to be used separately, in different parts of the factory. The controller also decides to account for the maintenance and repair services as non-lease components of the contract. Further, these services are considered to be distinct for each machine, and so are separate non-lease performance obligations.

The controller needs to allocate the $800,000 of consideration to the various lease and non-lease components. She notes that there are a number of local suppliers that provide similar maintenance and repair services for each of the machines, and that standalone prices can be found to separately lease the two machines. These standalone prices are noted in the following table:

	Lease	Maintenance	Totals
Stamping machine	$200,000	$30,000	$230,000
CNC machine	570,000	100,000	670,000
Totals	$770,000	$130,000	$900,000

The controller allocates the $800,000 consideration in the contract to the lease and non-lease components on a relative basis, employing their standalone prices. This results in the following allocation:

	Lease	Maintenance	Totals
Stamping machine	$177,778	$26,667	$204,445
CNC machine	506,667	88,888	595,555
Totals	$684,445	$115,555	$800,000

The consideration in a lease should be remeasured and reallocated when either of the following events occurs:

- The lease liability is remeasured. This could be triggered by a change in the term of the lease, or a revision to the assessment of whether a lease option will be exercised.
- There is a contract modification that is not being accounted for as a separate contract.

Lease Components (Lessor)

In general, a lessor allocates consideration to lease components in the same manner as the lessee. In addition, the lessor allocates any capitalized costs to the lease and non-lease components to which those costs relate. An example of a capitalized cost is the initial direct costs incurred to create a contract. Initial direct costs are discussed in the next section.

If a lessor receives a variable payment amount that relates to a lease component, it should recognize the payment as income in the same period as the one on which the variable payment was based.

EXAMPLE

Prickly Corporation leases space from Capital Inc., which it uses as a retail store to sell cacti and other thorny plants. Following the end of each month, Prickly is required to pay 2% of its revenue to Capital; this is the variable portion of the lease payment for the retail space. In early March, Prickly sends a payment of $540 to Capital, which is the variable portion of the payment, and which relates to its February sales. Capital should recognize this payment as income in its February income statement.

Prickly discloses in its financial statements the fixed amount of its operating lease cost, while separately disclosing the $540 as a variable lease cost.

Initial Direct Costs

Initial direct costs are those costs that are only incurred if a lease agreement occurs. This usually includes broker commissions and payments made to existing tenants to obtain a lease, because these costs are only incurred if a lease agreement is signed. Legal fees are usually not included, since the parties must pay their attorneys even if a lease arrangement falls through. Also, staff time spent working on a lease arrangement will be incurred irrespective of the lease agreement, and so is not considered part of initial direct costs.

Initial direct costs are capitalized at the inception of a lease, and are then amortized ratably over the term of the lease. Throughout the term of a lease, any unamortized initial direct costs are included in the measurement of the right-of-use asset (which is discussed later).

Lease Consideration

Consideration is defined as something of value that induces the parties to a contract to exchange mutual performances. The consideration in a leasing arrangement is most obviously the periodic fixed lease payments made by the lessee. Consideration can also include monthly service charges, as well as variable payments that are defined by an index or a rate. For example, a lease payment may be adjusted each year, based on changes in the consumer price index.

The Lease Term

One of the key components of a lease is the lease term. This is considered to be the noncancelable period of a lease, as well as the following additional periods that may apply:

- Lease extension options if it is reasonably certain that the lessee will exercise these options
- Lease termination options if it is reasonably certain that the lessee will not exercise these options
- Lease extension options where the lessor controls the options

An entity makes a judgment call as of the lease commencement date regarding which of the preceding factors will apply to the derivation of an estimated lease term. This judgment is based on those factors that create an economic incentive for the lessee. Examples of economic incentives are reduced lease payments in the optional period, the significance of any leasehold improvements, and the importance of the underlying asset to the lessee's operations.

EXAMPLE

Subatomic Research operates a laboratory in leased facilities. The laboratory has been designated as an airborne infection isolation room by the federal government, which is quite a difficult certification to obtain. The lease has an option for Subatomic to extend the lease term by five years. It is highly likely that Subatomic will renew the lease, given the high cost of moving elsewhere and then applying for recertification.

EXAMPLE

Newton Enterprises offers free science classes to high school students. These endeavors require Newton to lease training facilities. Its most recent lease is for 10 years, with a termination option after seven years. Annual lease payments are $100,000. If Newton terminates the lease, it must pay a $30,000 termination penalty. The managers of Newton conclude that it is not reasonably certain that Newton will need the facilities after seven years of use, especially considering the relatively small size of the termination penalty when compared to the amount of the annual lease payments. Consequently, Newton elects to measure the lease term as being seven years.

If the lessor provides a period of free rent, the lease term is considered to begin at the commencement date and to include all rent-free periods.

A lease term should not extend past the period when it is enforceable. A lease is no longer enforceable when both the lessee and the lessor can terminate the lease without permission from the other party, and by paying no more than an insignificant penalty.

A government entity that leases space may require that a fiscal funding clause be inserted into the lease. This clause allows the government to cancel a lease if it does not have sufficient funding. When this clause is present, the lease term should only include those periods for which there is a reasonable certainty of funding.

Initial Measurement of Lease Payments

There are a number of possible payments by a lessee that can be associated with a lease component. All of the following payments relate to the use of the underlying asset in a lease:

- Fixed payments, minus any lease incentives payable to the lessee
- Variable lease payments that depend on an index or a rate (such as the consumer price index)
- The exercise price of an option to purchase the underlying asset, if it is reasonably certain that the lessee will exercise the option
- Penalty payments associated with an assumed exercise of an option to terminate the lease
- Fees paid to the owners of a special-purpose entity for creating the transaction
- Residual value guarantees, if it is probable that these amounts will be owed. Note that a lease provision requiring the lessee to pay for any deficiency in residual value that is caused by damage or excessive usage is not considered a guarantee of the residual value.

At the commencement of a lease, a number of direct costs may also have been incurred. Examples of these costs are commissions and payments made to incentivize a tenant to terminate a lease. Costs that would have been incurred even in the absence of a lease (such as general overhead and salaries) are not direct costs.

A lessor might pay a third party for a guarantee of the residual value of an underlying asset. This payment is considered an executory cost of the contract; it is not considered part of the lease payments.

If there is a requirement in a lease agreement that the lessee dismantle and remove an underlying asset following the end of a lease, this cost is considered a lease payment.

Subsequent Measurement of Lease Payments

It is only necessary to reassess a lessee's option to purchase an underlying asset or the length of the lease term when one of the following events occurs subsequent to the initial measurement of a lease:

- *Contractual requirement*. An event occurs that was addressed in the contract, requiring the lessee to exercise (or not exercise) an option or terminate the lease.
- *No option exercise*. The lessee does not exercise an option despite a previous determination that it was reasonably certain for the lessee to do so.
- *Option exercise*. The lessee exercises an option despite a previous determination that it was reasonably certain that the lessee would not do so.
- *Significant event*. A significant event has occurred that is within the control of the lessee, and which directly affects the lessee's decision to exercise or not exercise an option, or to purchase the underlying asset. Examples of significant events are the construction of significant leasehold improvements that will be of value to the lessee during the option period, and making significant modifications to the underlying asset.

It is only necessary to remeasure the lease payments associated with a lease when one of the following events occurs:

- *Lease modification*. The initial lease is modified, and the modification is not accounted for as a separate contract.
- *Resolved contingency*. A contingency that had resulted in variable lease payments has now been resolved, so that the payments become fixed for the remainder of the lease term.
- *Other changes*. There is a change in the lease term, a change in the assessment of whether an option will be exercised, or a change in the probable amount that will be owed by the lessee under a residual value guarantee.

Types of Leases

There are several types of lease designations, which differ if an entity is the lessee or the lessor. It is critical to determine the type of a lease, since the accounting varies by lease type. The choices for a **lessee** are that a lease can be designated as either a finance lease or an operating lease. In essence, a *finance lease* designation implies that the lessee has purchased the underlying asset (even though this may not actually be the case), while an *operating lease* designation implies that the lessee has obtained the use of the underlying asset for only a period of time. A lessee should classify a lease as a finance lease when any of the following criteria are met:

- *Ownership transfer*. Ownership of the underlying asset is shifted to the lessee by the end of the lease term.

- *Ownership option.* The lessee has a purchase option to buy the leased asset, and is reasonably certain to use it.
- *Lease term.* The lease term covers the major part of the underlying asset's remaining economic life. This is considered to be 75% or more of the remaining economic life of the underlying asset. This criterion is not valid if the lease commencement date is near the end of the asset's economic life, which is considered to be a date that falls within the last 25% of the underlying asset's total economic life.
- *Present value.* The present value of the sum of all lease payments and any lessee-guaranteed residual value matches or exceeds the fair value of the underlying asset. The present value is based on the interest rate implicit in the lease.
- *Specialization.* The asset is so specialized that it has no alternative use for the lessor following the lease term. In this situation, there are essentially no remaining benefits that revert to the lessor.

When none of the preceding criteria are met, the lessee must classify a lease as an operating lease.

When the lessor is a government entity, the underlying asset may be a more substantial facility, such as an airport, where it is impossible to determine an economic life or the fair value of the asset. For these reasons, such leases should be considered operating leases. All of the following conditions should apply before a lease from a government entity is considered an operating lease:

- *Ownership.* The underlying asset is owned by a government entity, and ownership cannot be transferred to the lessee.
- *Nature of the asset.* The underlying asset is part of a larger facility, such as an airport, and is a permanent structure that cannot be moved.
- *Termination right.* The lessor has the right to terminate the lease at any time.

The choices for a **lessor** are that a lease can be designated as a *sales-type lease*, *direct finance lease*, or *operating lease*. If all of the preceding conditions just noted for a lessee's finance lease are met by a lease, then the lessor designates it as a sales-type lease (in effect, an asset is being sold to the lessee). If this is not the case, then the lessor has a choice of designating a lease as either a direct financing lease (in effect, the lessor earns interest income from its leasing activities) or an operating lease.

The lessor should designate any remaining lease as a direct financing lease when both of the following criteria are met:

- *Present value.* The present value of the lease payments and any residual asset value that is guaranteed by the lessee or any other party matches or exceeds substantially all of the fair value of the underlying asset. In this context, "substantially" means 90% or more of the fair value of the underlying asset. The present value is based on the rate implicit in the lease.

- *Collection probability*. The lessor will probably collect the lease payments, as well as any additional amount needed to satisfy the residual value guarantee.

When none of these additional criteria are met, the lessor classifies a lease as an operating lease.

Asset and Liability Recognition (Lessee)

A central concept of the accounting for leases is that the lessee should recognize the assets and liabilities that underlie each leasing arrangement. This concept results in the following recognition in the balance sheet of the lessee as of the lease commencement date:

- Recognize a liability to make lease payments to the lessor
- Recognize a right-of-use asset that represents the right of the lessee to use the leased asset during the lease term

There are a number of sub-topics related to asset and liability recognition, which are stated in the following sub-sections.

Initial Measurement

As of the commencement date of a lease, the lessee measures the liability and the right-of-use asset associated with the lease. These measurements are derived as follows:

- *Lease liability*. The present value of the lease payments, discounted at the discount rate for the lease. This rate is the rate implicit in the lease when that rate is readily determinable. If not, the lessee instead uses its incremental borrowing rate.
- *Right-of-use asset*. The initial amount of the lease liability, plus any lease payments made to the lessor before the lease commencement date, plus any initial direct costs incurred, minus any lease incentives received.

EXAMPLE

Inscrutable Corporation enters into a five-year lease, where the lease payments are $35,000 per year, payable at the end of each year. Inscrutable incurs initial direct costs of $8,000. The rate implicit in the lease is 8%.

At the commencement of the lease, the lease liability is $139,745, which is calculated as $35,000 multiplied by the 3.9927 rate for the five-period present value of an ordinary annuity. The right-of-use asset is calculated as the lease liability plus the amount of the initial direct costs, for a total of $147,745.

Short-Term Leases

When a lease has a term of 12 months or less, the lessee can elect not to recognize lease-related assets and liabilities in the balance sheet. This election is made by class of asset. When a lessee makes this election, it should usually recognize the expense related to a lease on a straight-line basis over the term of the lease.

If the lease term changes so that the remaining term now extends more than 12 months beyond the end of the previously determined lease term or the lessee will likely purchase the underlying asset, the arrangement is no longer considered a short-term lease. In this situation, account for the lease as a longer-term lease as of the date when there was a change in circumstances.

Finance Leases

When a lessee has designated a lease as a finance lease, it should recognize the following over the term of the lease:

- The ongoing amortization of the right-of-use asset
- The ongoing amortization of the interest on the lease liability
- Any variable lease payments that are not included in the lease liability
- Any impairment of the right-of-use asset

The amortization period for the right-of-use asset is from the lease commencement date to the earlier of the end of the lease term or the end of the useful life of the asset. An exception is when it is reasonably certain that the lessee will exercise an option to purchase the asset, in which case the amortization period is through the end of the asset's useful life.

After the commencement date, the lessee increases the carrying amount of the lease liability to include the interest expense on the lease liability, while reducing the carrying amount by the amount of all lease payments made during the period. The interest on the lease liability is the amount that generates a constant periodic discount rate on the remaining liability balance.

After the commencement date, the lessee reduces the right-of-use asset by the amount of accumulated amortization and accumulated impairment (if any).

EXAMPLE

Giro Cabinetry agrees to a five-year lease of equipment that requires an annual $20,000 payment, due at the end of each year. At the end of the lease period, Giro has the option to buy the equipment for $1,000. Since the expected residual value of the equipment at that time is expected to be $25,000, the large discount makes it reasonably certain that the purchase option will be exercised. At the commencement date of the lease, the fair value of the equipment is $120,000, with an economic life of eight years. The discount rate for the lease is 6%.

Giro classifies the lease as a finance lease, since it is reasonably certain to exercise the purchase option.

The lease liability at the commencement date is $84,995, which is calculated as the present value of five payments of $20,000, plus the present value of the $1,000 purchase option payment, discounted at 6%. Giro recognizes the right-of-use asset as the same amount, since there are no initial direct costs, lease incentives, or other types of payments made by Giro, either at or before the commencement date.

Giro amortizes the right-of-use asset over the eight-year expected useful life of the equipment, under the assumption that it will exercise the purchase option and therefore keep the equipment for the eight-year period.

As an example of the subsequent accounting for the lease, Giro recognizes a first-year interest expense of $5,100 (calculated as 6% × $84,995 lease liability), and recognizes the amortization of the right-of-use asset in the amount of $10,624 (calculated as $84,995 ÷ 8 years). This results in a lease liability at the end of Year 1 that has been reduced to $70,095 (calculated as $84,995 + $5,100 interest - $20,000 lease payment) and a right-of-use asset that has been reduced to $74,371 (calculated as $84,995 - $10,624 amortization).

By the end of Year 5, which is when the lease terminates, the lease liability has been reduced to $1,000, which is the amount of the purchase option. Giro exercises the option, which settles the remaining liability. At that time, the carrying amount of the right-of-use asset has declined to $31,875 (reflecting five years of amortization at $10,624 per year). Giro shifts this amount into a fixed asset account, and depreciates it over the remaining three years of its useful life.

Operating Leases

When a lessee has designated a lease as an operating lease, the lessee should recognize the following over the term of the lease:

- A lease cost in each period, where the total cost of the lease is allocated over the lease term on a straight-line basis. This can be altered if there is another systematic and rational basis of allocation that more closely follows the benefit usage pattern to be derived from the underlying asset.
- Any variable lease payments that are not included in the lease liability
- Any impairment of the right-of-use asset

EXAMPLE

Nuance Corporation enters into an operating lease in which the lease payment is $25,000 per year for the first five years and $30,000 per year for the next five years. These payments sum to $275,000 over ten years. Nuance will therefore recognize a lease expense of $27,500 per year for all of the years in the lease term.

At any point in the life of an operating lease, the remaining cost of the lease is considered to be the total lease payments, plus all initial direct costs associated with the lease, minus the lease cost already recognized in previous periods.

After the commencement date, the lessee measures the lease liability at the present value of the lease payments that have not yet been made, using the same discount rate that was established at the commencement date.

After the commencement date, the lessee measures the right-of-use asset at the amount of the lease liability, adjusted for the following items:

- Any impairment of the asset
- Prepaid or accrued lease payments
- Any remaining balance of lease incentives received
- Any unamortized initial direct costs

EXAMPLE

Hubble Corporation enters into a 10-year operating lease for its corporate offices. The annual lease payment is $40,000 to be paid at the end of each year. The company incurs initial direct costs of $8,000, and receives $15,000 from the lessor as a lease incentive. Hubble's incremental borrowing rate is 6%. The initial direct costs and lease incentive will be amortized over the 10 years of the lease term.

Hubble measures the lease liability as the present value of the 10 lease payments at a 6% discount rate, which is $294,404. The right-of-use asset is measured at $287,404, which is the initial $294,404 measurement, plus the initial direct costs of $8,000, minus the lease incentive of $15,000.

After one year, the carrying amount of the lease liability is $272,068, which is the present value of the remaining nine lease payments at a 6% discount rate. The carrying amount of the right-of-use asset is $265,768, which is the amount of the liability, plus the unamortized initial direct costs of $7,200, minus the remaining balance of the lease incentive of $13,500.

Optional Lease Payments

When there is an optional payment in a lease agreement that can be made by the lessee to purchase a leased asset, this optional payment is only included in the recognition of assets and liabilities if it is reasonably certain that the lessee will exercise the purchase option.

Right-of-Use Asset Impairment

If a right-of-use asset is determined to be impaired, the impairment is immediately recorded, thereby reducing the carrying amount of the asset. Its subsequent measurement is calculated as the carrying amount immediately after the impairment transaction, minus any subsequent accumulated amortization.

EXAMPLE

Horton Corporation enters into a five-year equipment lease that is classified as an operating lease. At the end of Year 2, when the carrying amount of the lease liability and the right-of-use asset are both $100,000, the controller determines that the asset is impaired, and recognizes an impairment loss of $70,000. This reduces the carrying amount of the asset to $30,000.

Beginning in Year 3 and continuing through the remainder of the lease term, Horton amortizes the right-of-use asset at a rate of $10,000 per year, which will bring the carrying amount of the asset to zero by the end of the lease term.

Leasehold Improvement Amortization

A leasehold improvement is a customization of rented property, such as the addition of carpeting, cabinetry, lighting, and walls. This asset should be amortized over the shorter of the remaining lease term and its useful life. The one exception is when it is reasonably certain that the lessee will take possession of the underlying asset at the end of the lease, in which case the amortization period is through the end of the asset's useful life.

Subleases

A sublease occurs when a lessee leases the underlying asset to a third party. A sublease agreement typically arises when the original tenant no longer needs to use leased space or can no longer afford to make the lease payments. This situation is most common for commercial properties, but can arise for residential properties as well. The following accounting can apply to this situation:

- *Operating lease.* If a lease is classified as an operating lease, the original lessee continues to account for it in the same manner that it did before the commencement of the sublease.
- *Conversion from finance lease.* If the original lease was classified as a finance lease and the sublease is classified as either a sales-type or direct financing lease, then the original lessee must derecognize the right-of-use asset on its books. The accounting for the original lease liability remains the same.
- *Conversion from operating lease.* If the original lease was classified as an operating lease and the sublease is classified as either a sales-type lease or a direct financing lease, then the original lessee must derecognize the right-of-use asset on its books, and account for the original lease liability as of the sublease commencement date as though it were a finance lease (see the preceding Finance Leases sub-section).

Maintenance Deposits

A lessee may be required to pay the lessor a maintenance deposit, which the lessor retains if the lessee damages the property during the lease term. If it is probable that the lessor will retain this deposit at the end of the lease, the lessee should recognize the payment as a variable lease expense.

Derecognition

At the termination of a lease, the right-of-use asset and associated lease liability are removed from the books. The difference between the two amounts is accounted for as a profit or loss at that time. If the lessee purchases the underlying asset at the termination of a lease, then any difference between the purchase price and the lease liability is recorded as an adjustment to the asset's carrying amount.

If a lessee subleases an underlying asset and the terms of the original agreement then relieve the lessee of the primary lease obligation, this is considered a termination of the original lease.

Lease Recognition Topics (Lessor)

The accounting for leases by lessors varies in several respects from the accounting by lessees. In particular, there are more classifications of leases for a lessor; there are sales-type leases, direct financing leases, and operating leases. The accounting for these leases is addressed in the following sub-sections.

Sales-Type Leases

In a sales-type lease, the lessor is assumed to actually be selling a product to the lessee, which calls for the recognition of a profit or loss on the sale. Consequently, this results in the following accounting at the commencement date of the lease:

- *Derecognize asset.* The lessor derecognizes the underlying asset, since it is assumed to have been sold to the lessee.
- *Recognize net investment.* The lessor recognizes a net investment in the lease. This investment includes the following:
    - The present value of lease payments not yet received
    - The present value of the guaranteed amount of the underlying asset's residual value at the end of the lease term
    - The present value of the unguaranteed amount of the underlying asset's residual value at the end of the lease term
- *Recognize profit or loss.* The lessor recognizes any selling profit or loss caused by the lease.
- *Recognize initial direct costs.* The lessor recognizes any initial direct costs as an expense, if there is a difference between the carrying amount of the underlying asset and its fair value. If the fair value of the underlying asset is instead equal to its carrying amount, then defer the initial direct costs and include them in the measurement of the lessor's investment in the lease.

In addition, the lessor must account for the following items subsequent to the commencement date of the lease:

- *Interest income*. The ongoing amount of interest earned on the net investment in the lease.
- *Variable lease payments*. If there are any variable lease payments that were not included in the net investment in the lease, record them in profit or loss in the same reporting period as the events that triggered the payments.
- *Impairment*. Recognize any impairment of the net investment in the lease.
- *Net investment*. Adjust the balance of the net investment in the lease by adding interest income and subtracting any lease payments collected during the period.

However, if the collectability of the lease payments and payments related to a residual value guarantee are not probable as of the commencement date, the lessor should not derecognize the underlying asset. Instead, the lessor recognizes lease payments (including variable lease payments) as a deposit liability as they are received. This treatment continues until the earlier of either of these events:

- *Probable collectability*. It becomes probable that lease payments and payments related to a residual value guarantee will be collectible.
- *Contract termination*. Either of the following occurs:
    - The contract has been terminated *and* the lease payments received to date are not refundable; or
    - The lessor has repossessed the underlying asset, *and* has no further obligation to the lessee, *and* the lease payments received to date are not refundable.

When the collectability of payments from a lessee was initially considered to not be probable, but this assessment was later changed, the lessor should take the following steps as of the latter event:

- *Derecognize asset*. Derecognize the carrying amount of the underlying asset.
- *Derecognize liability*. If there is a deposit liability, derecognize it.
- *Recognize net investment*. Recognize a net investment in the lease. This amount is derived from the remaining lease payments, the remaining lease term, and the rate implicit in the lease at the commencement date.
- *Recognize profit or loss*. Recognize any selling profit or loss, which is calculated as the lease receivable plus the carrying amount of the deposit liability, minus the carrying amount of the underlying asset, net of the unguaranteed residual asset.

If this type of lease is terminated before the end of its lease term, the lessor must test the net investment in the lease for impairment and recognize an impairment loss if necessary. Then reclassify the net investment in the lease to the most appropriate fixed asset category. The reclassified asset is recorded at the sum of the carrying amounts of the lease receivable and the residual asset.

At the end of the lease term, the lessor reclassifies its net investment in the lease to the most appropriate fixed asset account.

EXAMPLE

Capital Inc. enters into an eight-year lease of equipment with a lessee. Under the terms of the agreement, Capital will receive an annual lease payment of $10,000, payable at the end of each year. The lessee also provides Capital with a residual value guarantee of $15,000. Upon reviewing the credit rating of the lessee, Capital's controller concludes that it is probable that Capital will collect the lease payments and any additional funding necessary to satisfy the lessee's residual value guarantee. Additional pertinent facts are:

- The equipment has a 10-year estimated economic life
- The equipment has a carrying amount of $60,000
- The equipment has a fair value of $71,509 at the commencement date
- The expected residual value of the equipment is $18,000 at the end of the lease term
- There is no transfer of equipment ownership to the lessee, nor is there a purchase option
- The rate implicit in the lease is 6%

The controller classifies the lease as a sales-type lease, because the combined present value of the lease payments and the residual value guaranteed by the lessee is $71,509, which is substantially all of the fair value of the underlying asset.

The controller measures the net investment in the lease at $73,391 at the commencement date of the lease; this equals the fair value of the equipment. This net investment consists of the following:

Present value of eight lease payments of $10,000 each	$62,098
Present value of $15,000 residual value guarantee	9,411
Present value of the $3,000 unguaranteed residual value	1,882
Net investment in the lease	$73,391

The selling profit on the lease is $13,391, which is the difference between the lease receivable (the present values of the lease payments and the guaranteed residual value) and the carrying amount of the equipment net of the unguaranteed residual asset. The calculation is:

Lease receivable (present values of lease payments and guaranteed residual value)	$71,509
- Carrying amount of the equipment net of the present value of the unguaranteed residual asset	58,118
Selling profit	$13,391

At the lease commencement date, the controller derecognizes the $60,000 carrying amount of the equipment, recognizes the net investment in the lease of $73,391, and recognizes the selling profit of $13,391.

At the end of the first year of the lease, Capital receives and recognizes the annual $10,000 lease payment. Capital also recognizes interest on the net investment in the lease, which is $4,403 (calculated as $73,391 net investment in the lease × 6% rate implicit in the lease). This results in a reduced balance of $67,794 in the net investment in the lease, which is calculated as the $73,391 beginning balance, plus the $4,403 interest income, minus the $10,000 lease payment.

Direct Financing Leases

In a direct financing lease, the lessor acquires assets and leases them to its customers, with the intent of generating revenue from the resulting interest payments. At the commencement date of a direct financing lease, the lessor engages in the following activities:

- Recognize the net investment in the lease. This includes the selling profit and any initial direct costs for which recognition is deferred.
- Recognize a selling loss caused by the lease arrangement, if this has occurred
- Derecognize the underlying asset

In addition, the lessor must account for the following items subsequent to the commencement date of the lease:

- *Interest income.* Record the ongoing amount of interest earned on the net investment in the lease.
- *Variable lease payments.* If there are any variable lease payments that were not included in the net investment in the lease, record them in profit or loss in the same reporting period as the events that triggered the payments.
- *Impairment.* Record any impairment of the net investment in the lease.
- *Net investment.* Adjust the balance of the net investment in the lease by adding interest income and subtracting any lease payments collected during the period.

If this type of lease is terminated before the end of its lease term, the lessor must test the net investment in the lease for impairment and recognize an impairment loss if necessary. Then reclassify the net investment in the lease to the most appropriate fixed asset category. The reclassified asset is recorded at the sum of the carrying amounts of the lease receivable and the residual asset.

At the end of the lease term, the lessor reclassifies its net investment in the lease to the most appropriate fixed asset account.

Operating Leases

An operating lease is any lease other than a sales-type lease or a direct financing lease. At the commencement date of an operating lease, the lessor shall defer all initial direct costs. In addition, the lessor must account for the following items subsequent to the commencement date of the lease:

- *Lease payments*. Lease payments are recognized in profit or loss over the term of the lease on a straight-line basis, unless another systematic and rational basis more clearly represents the benefit that the lessee is deriving from the underlying asset. Profits cannot be recognized at the beginning of an operating lease, since control of the underlying asset has not been transferred to the lessee.
- *Variable lease payments*. If there are any variable lease payments, record them in profit or loss in the same reporting period as the events that triggered the payments.
- *Initial direct costs*. Recognize initial direct costs as an expense over the term of the lease, using the same recognition basis that was used for the recognition of lease income.

If the collectability of the lease payments and payments related to a residual value guarantee are not probable as of the commencement date, the lessor limits the recognition of lease income to the lesser of the payments described in the immediately preceding bullet points or the actual lease payments (including variable lease payments) that have been received. If this assessment later changes, any difference between the income that should have been recognized and which had been recognized is recognized in the current period.

EXAMPLE

Scottish Colonial Leasing enters into a five-year lease where the annual lease payments begin at $5,000 and escalate by $500 for each of the next four years. There are initial direct costs of $2,000. The collectability of lease payments is not probable, so Scottish classifies the lease as an operating lease.

Since the lease is classified as an operating lease, Scottish continues to measure the underlying asset as a fixed asset. Due to the risk of nonpayment, Scottish only recognizes lease income when payments are received from the lessee, and in the amount of those payments. Thus, when the first year payment of $5,000 is received, Scottish recognizes lease income of $5,000.

Scottish recognizes 20% of the initial direct costs in each year, which is a $400 expense recognition per year.

> **Note:** There can be some confusion about the treatment of operating leases from the perspectives of the lessor and the lessee. The lessor does *not* capitalize an operating lease (only the underlying asset), while a lessee (with some exceptions) capitalizes the related right-of-use asset.

Variable Lease Payments

Most variable lease payments should be excluded from the recognition of lease assets and liabilities. However, lease payments that depend on an index or a rate should be included in this recognition.

Any variable charges to a lessee that are essentially a reimbursement of the lessor's costs are not considered part of a lease. For example, a lessor may require a lessee to pay the real estate taxes on a leased property, or the associated building insurance. Neither variable payment is for the right to use the underlying asset and does not depend on an index or a rate, and so is not a component of the contract.

In addition, a payment that is called a variable payment, but which is in reality a fixed payment should be included in the recognition of a leased asset or liability.

Lease Modifications

When a contract is modified, the change is accounted for as a separate contract, but only when both of the following conditions are present:

- *Additional right of use*. The lessee is granted an additional right of use as part of the modification.
- *Incremental price*. There is an incremental increase in the lease price that is commensurate with the standalone price of the additional right of use that is being granted, adjusted for the contract-specific circumstances.

EXAMPLE

Grunge Motor Sports needs additional warehouse space for the storage of its dirt bike products. The lessor of its current warehouse has adjacent warehouse space, which is added onto the current lease. The lease price for this additional space is less than the current market rate in the area, because the lessor did not have to incur several additional charges that it normally would have paid for an entirely new client. It will be accounted for as a separate contract.

EXAMPLE

Monk Books currently leases 30,000 square feet of space for its scriptorium, and is in the 6th year of a 10-year lease. Given the increased demand for hand-illuminated books, Monk enters into a lease modification with the lessor, which adds 15,000 more square feet to the scriptorium as of the beginning of the 7th year at the then-current market rate.

Monk's controller accounts for the modification as a new contract, since Monk is being granted an additional right of use in excess of the original contract. The new contract only includes the incremental change noted in the lease modification.

If these two conditions are not present, then the existing lease classification is re-assessed as of the date of the contract modification. This reassessment encompasses the modified terms and conditions, as well as the facts and circumstances of the situation as of that date. For example, the fair value of the underlying asset might have changed between the initial contract date and the modification date.

Lessee Impact

When there is a contract modification, the lessee should reallocate the consideration remaining in the contract to the lease components, and also remeasure the lease liability with a discount rate for the lease that is derived as of the effective date of the contract modification. These changes should only be made when a contract modification causes any of the following to occur:

- An additional right of use is granted to the lessee. This adjusts the amount of the right-of-use asset.
- Alters the term of the lease. This adjusts the amount of the right-of-use asset.
- Either fully or partially terminates the existing lease. This decreases the carrying amount of the right-of-use asset proportionally, based on the amount of lease termination. If this causes a difference between the revised lease liability and the right-of-use asset, the difference is recognized as a gain or loss as of the effective date of the modification.
- Alters the amount of the consideration in the contract. This adjusts the amount of the right-of-use asset.

EXAMPLE

Lethal Sushi and its landlord agree to extend the existing 5-year lease on a restaurant location to 8 years, thereby adding three years to the existing lease. The modified lease also increases the amount of the lease payments for the three years that have been added. This change is not considered a new contract, since no additional right of use has been granted. The only accounting issue is to remeasure the amount of the remaining lease liability, given the presence of the additional (and larger) payments. The increased amount of the lease liability is also recorded as an adjustment to the right-of-use asset.

EXAMPLE

For another restaurant location, Lethal Sushi also agrees to modify an existing lease. However, in this case Lethal obtains the use of a nearby building, so an additional right of use has been granted. The lease modification incorporates a substantial discount for the nearby building, at a rate that is 40% below the current market rate for similar properties. Because the price stated in the modification is not commensurate with the standalone price of the additional right of use, this modification cannot be treated as a separate contract. Instead, the company's controller allocates the lease payments in the modified contract to the two lease components on a relative standalone price basis, based on the remaining lease terms associated with each component. This remaining lease cost will be recognized over the respective lease terms of each lease component on a straight-line basis.

EXAMPLE

Country Fresh Produce enters into a 5-year lease for 20,000 square feet of office space. The lease payments are fixed at $100,000 per year. The original discount rate for the lease was 8%. The lease is classified as an operating lease. At the beginning of Year 3, Country Fresh and the lessor agree to modify the original lease for the remaining three years by reducing the lease payments by $10,000 per year. Since only the lease payments are being modified, this alteration cannot be accounted for as a separate contract, nor does the lease classification change.

These changes call for a remeasurement of the lease liability, based on the following information:

- Remaining lease term is three years
- Payments of $90,000 in each year, from Year 3 through Year 5
- Country Fresh's incremental borrowing rate is 6% as of the effective date of the modification

The remeasured lease liability is $240,570, which is $17,140 less than the $257,710 pre-modification lease liability. Country Fresh treats the $17,140 as a reduction in the right-of-use asset.

As of the date of the modification, the remaining lease cost for Country Fresh is $270,000, which is the sum of the remaining three payments of $90,000 each. The lease liability on Country Fresh's balance sheet in the following years will be as indicated in the following table:

Beginning of	Lease Liability	Derivation
Year 3	$240,570	[Ordinary annuity factor for 3 years] 2.6730 × $90,000
Year 4	165,006	[Ordinary annuity factor for 2 years] 1.8334 × $90,000
Year 5	84,906	[Ordinary annuity factor for 1 year] 0.9434 × $90,000

Lessor Impact

When there is a contract modification and it is not accounted for as a separate contract, the lessor accounts for the change as though the original lease was cancelled and replaced by a new lease as of the effective date of the modification. Those changes are as follows:

- *Operating lease treatment.* If a lease has been classified as an operating lease, any prepaid or accrued lease rentals associated with the original lease are now considered to be part of the payments associated with the modified lease.
- *Direct financing or sales-type lease.* If a lease has been classified as a direct financing or sales-type lease, derecognize the accrued rent asset or deferred rent liability; then adjust the selling profit or loss to match the amount of the derecognition.

EXAMPLE

Capital Inc. enters into a 5-year operating lease as the lessor. The lease is for 5,000 square feet of prime office space, for which the annual lease payment is $100,000. This amount increases by 5% in each subsequent year, which results in the following schedule of lease payments:

Year	Lease Payment
1	$100,000
2	105,000
3	110,250
4	115,763
5	121,551
Total	$552,564
Average	$110,513

At the beginning of Year 3, both parties agree to modify the lease for the remaining three years to include an additional 2,000 square feet of office space, which results in a new annual lease payment of $130,000, and which then increases by 5% in each subsequent year. The incremental increase in the lease payment represents a substantial reduction from the market rate for this type of property. Because the pricing of the modification is not commensurate with the standalone price, the modification is not treated as an entirely new lease. Instead, Capital Inc. accounts for the modified lease on a go-forward basis with the following inputs:

- Total lease payments yet to be made of $409,825 (calculated as $130,000 + $136,500 + $143,325)
- At the beginning of Year 3, Capital Inc. has an accrued lease rental asset of $16,026 (calculated as $110,513 annual average lease income × 2 years, minus lease payments of $100,000 and $105,000).

Capital Inc. subtracts the accrued lease rental asset of $16,026 from the $409,825 total lease payments yet to be made to arrive at $393,799 of lease income to be recognized over the remaining three years of the lease. This is recognized on a straight-line basis, at $131,266 per year.

If a modified lease was originally classified as a direct financing lease, and the modification is not accounted for as a separate contract, the modified lease is accounted for by the lessor as follows:

- *Continues as direct financing lease.* If the classification of the lease continues to be as a direct financing lease, the discount rate for the lease is adjusted in order to have the initial net investment in the modified lease equal the carrying amount of the net investment in the original lease just before the effective date of the lease modification. The same accounting applies if a sales-type lease is modified to be a direct financing lease.

EXAMPLE

Capital Inc. is the lessor in an existing leasing arrangement, which is about to be modified. The lease is classified as a direct financing lease, and will continue to be classified in that manner after the modification has been completed. The carrying amount of Capital's net investment in the lease is $62,000 just before the effective date of the lease modification. The modification will shorten the term of the lease, which increases the residual value of the underlying asset to $40,000. In order to have the $62,000 carrying amount of the investment equal its $40,000 residual value by the end of the lease period, Capital must calculate the interest rate that will generate interest income on the net investment over the remaining four-year term of the lease. Using a derived interest rate of 10.3775%, that calculation is:

Year	Beginning Balance	Interest Income	Ending Balance
1	$62,000	$6,434	$55,566
2	55,566	5,766	49,800
3	49,800	5,168	44,632
4	44,632	4,632	40,000

- *Reclassified as sales-type lease.* If the classification of the lease is altered to be a sales-type lease, it is subsequently accounted for as a sales-type lease. To calculate the selling profit or loss associated with the lease, the fair value of the underlying asset is derived as of the effective date of the lease modification, and the carrying amount of the net investment in the original lease is that value just prior to the effective date of the modification.

EXAMPLE

Capital Inc. is the lessor in a leasing arrangement that was originally classified as a direct financing lease, because the lease covered only a reduced portion of the economic life of the underlying asset. The lease is then modified to extend the lease term, which now encompasses such a large proportion of the economic life of the asset that the lease is reclassified as a sales-type lease. In effect, Capital is now assumed to be selling the asset to the lessee.

At the effective date of the modification, Capital derecognizes the carrying amount of the net investment in the original direct financing lease, which is $71,500. Capital then recognizes a net investment in the sales-type lease of $75,000, which is the fair value of the underlying asset on the effective date of the modification. The $3,500 difference between these two values is the selling profit earned by Capital on the modified lease.

- *Reclassified as operating lease.* If the classification of the lease is altered to an operating lease, the carrying amount of the underlying asset is the same as the net investment in the original lease just prior to the effective date of the modification. The same accounting applies if a sales-type lease is modified to be an operating lease.

EXAMPLE

Capital Inc. is the lessor in a leasing arrangement that had originally been classified as a direct financing lease. The lease is then modified, resulting in a reclassification to an operating lease. Just prior to the effective date of the modification, Capital's net investment in the lease is $132,000. Capital derecognizes this net investment, and recognizes the underlying asset as a fixed asset in the same amount. The lease payments are $20,000 annually for the next five years. Capital recognizes these payments on a straight-line basis over the remaining years of the lease. Capital also depreciates the underlying asset during those five years.

Elections

There are several elections that an organization can use to simplify the accounting for leases. One option is to use a risk-free discount rate for present value calculations, rather than having to justify some other rate. Another election is to include non-leasing components in a leasing arrangement, thereby reducing the number of elements within a contract to which costs may be assigned. These two options are explained within this section. In addition, a lessee can elect not to recognize lease-related assets and liabilities in the balance sheet when a lease has a term of 12 months or less. This option was explained earlier in the Asset and Liability Recognition section.

Discount Rate

A business that is not publicly-held can elect to use a risk-free discount rate when deriving the present value of a lease. If so, this discount rate should be determined using a period comparable to that of the lease term. This election can be made by class of underlying asset, rather than at an entity-wide level. If a business makes this risk-free rate election, it must disclose the asset classes to which it has been applied.

When the rate implicit in a lease can be readily determined, the lessee must use that rate, rather than the risk-free rate, even if it has elected to use the risk-free rate election.

Separation of Non-Lease Components

A leasing arrangement may contain non-leasing components. For example, a lease contract might include a maintenance contract under which the lessor provides ongoing servicing of the leased asset. In this case, the consideration stated in the contract is to be allocated by the lessee to these separate parts based on their relative standalone prices. The accounting for non-leasing contract components will vary depending on their nature; it is not covered by the leasing standard.

A lessee can choose to not separate non-lease components from lease components. Instead, it can account for a lease component and any non-lease components associated with that lease component as a single lease component. This election must be made by class of asset; it is not available for just a single lease.

EXHIBIT

The Slot Master Casino leases two slot machines from Winner Manufacturing, along with maintenance services, for a total of $80,000. The two slot machines are of different types, and so will be accounted for as separate leases. Slot Master has made an accounting policy election to combine non-lease and lease components for its slot machines. This means that there are only two lease components in the contract, with no non-lease components.

The controller of Slot Master can easily find standalone prices for combinations of slot machines and maintenance services. These amounts are noted in the following table, along with the allocation of the $80,000 total contract price that is based on their standalone prices:

	Standalone Price	Allocated Price
Video slot machine lease & maintenance	$40,000	$36,364
Mechanical slot machine lease & maintenance	48,000	43,636
Totals	$88,000	$80,000

This option is also available to lessors, who can choose to not separate non-lease components from lease components. Instead, lessors can account for a lease component and any non-lease components associated with that lease component as a single lease component. This option is only available to the lessor if the timing and pattern of transfer of the non-lease component is the same as that of the lease component, and if the lease component would be classified as an operating lease.

Definition of Fair Value

If a lessor is not a manufacturer or a dealer, the fair value of the underlying asset at the commencement of a lease is considered to be its cost, where the cost used reflects any volume or trade discounts that may apply. However, if there has been a significant lapse of time between the purchase of the underlying asset and the commencement of the lease, then the normal definition of fair value shall apply.

Sale and Leaseback Transactions

A sale and leaseback transaction occurs when the seller transfers an asset to the buyer, and then leases the asset from the buyer. This arrangement most commonly occurs when the seller needs the funds associated with the asset being sold, despite still needing to occupy the space.

When such a transaction occurs, the first accounting step is to determine whether the transaction was at fair value. This can be judged from either of the following comparisons:

- Compare the difference between the sale price of the asset and its fair value.
- Compare the present value of the lease payments and the present value of market rental payments. This can include an estimation of any variable lease payments reasonably expected to be made.

If this comparison results in the determination that a sale and leaseback transaction is not at fair value, the entity must adjust the sale price on the same basis just used to determine whether the transaction was at fair value. This can result in the following adjustments:

- Any increase to the asset's sale price is accounted for as a rent prepayment
- Any reduction of the asset's sale price is accounted for as additional financing provided to the seller-lessee by the buyer-lessor. The seller-lessee should adjust the interest rate on this liability to ensure that:
  - o Interest on the liability is not greater than the principal payments over the shorter of the lease term and the financing term; and
  - o The carrying amount of the asset is not greater than the carrying amount of the liability at the earlier of the termination date of the lease or the date when asset control switches to the buyer-lessor.

In this arrangement, the consideration paid for the asset is accounted for as a financing transaction by both parties. However, if there is a repurchase option under which the seller can later buy back the asset, then the initial transaction cannot be considered a sale. The only exceptions are when:

- There are alternative assets readily available in the marketplace, and
- The price at which the option can be exercised is the fair value of the asset on the option exercise date.

If a sale and leaseback transaction is not considered a sale, then the seller-lessee cannot derecognize the asset, and accounts for any amounts received as a liability. Also, the buyer-lessor does not recognize the transferred asset, and accounts for any amount paid as a receivable.

EXAMPLE

Epic Rest Hotels sells one of its hotel properties to Capital Inc. The sale price is a cash payment of $7 million. At the same time as the sale, Epic Rest enters into a contract with Capital for the right to use the hotel for the next 10 years, in exchange for annual payments of $800,000, payable in arrears. Additional facts are:

- Immediately prior to the transaction, the hotel had a carrying amount on Epic's books of $6 million
- The fair value of the hotel is $7 million
- Capital obtains legal title to the property
- Capital has significant risks and rewards of ownership, such as the risk of loss if the property value declines
- The transaction is classified as an operating lease

As of the transaction commencement date, Epic Rest derecognizes the $6 million carrying amount of the hotel property, recognizes the $7 million cash receipt, and recognizes a $1 million gain on sale of the hotel. Also as of this date, Capital recognizes the hotel at a cost of $7 million.

Lease Presentation

The following presentation issues related to leases must be followed by the *lessee* in its financial statements:

Balance Sheet

- Right-of-use assets related to finance leases and operating leases are to be reported separately and not included with other assets. If these amounts are aggregated into other line items, disclose the line items in which they are located.
- Lease liabilities related to finance leases and operating leases are to be reported separately and not included with other assets. If these amounts are aggregated into other line items, disclose the line items in which they are located.
- Right-of-use assets for finance leases cannot be presented in the same line as right-of-use assets for operating leases
- Lease liabilities for finance leases cannot be presented in the same line as lease liabilities for operating leases.

Statement of Comprehensive Income

- The interest expense on the lease liability for finance leases does not have to be presented as a separate line item.
- The amortization expense for right-of-use assets does not have to be presented as a separate line item.

- The lease expense for operating leases should be included within the income from continuing operations section.

Statement of Cash Flows

- Repayments of the principal portion of the lease liability associated with financing leases are to be reported within the financing activities classification.
- Payments related to operating leases are to be reported within the operating activities classification.

The following presentation issues related to leases must be followed by the *lessor* in its financial statements:

Balance Sheet

- The aggregate amount of the lessor's net investment in sales-type leases and direct financing leases is presented separately from other assets.

Statement of Comprehensive Income

- Disclose the income arising from sales-type and direct financing leases (or do so in the accompanying footnotes). If this information is not separately presented in the statement of comprehensive income, note the line items in which it is located.
- There are several ways to present the profits or losses associated with the lessor's leasing activity for sales-type and direct financing leases. For example:
  - ○ If leases are used to provide financing to lessees (a direct finance lease), present the profit or loss in a single line item.
  - ○ If leases are used as a way to derive value from goods that would otherwise be sold (a sales-type lease), present in separate line items the revenue and cost of goods sold related to these leases. In this case, the amount of revenue recognized is the lesser of the fair value of the underlying asset at the commencement date and the sum of the lease receivable and any prepaid lease payments. The derivation of the cost of goods sold is the carrying amount of the underlying asset at the commencement date, minus the unguaranteed residual asset.

Statement of Cash Flows

- Cash receipts from all types of leases are classified by the lessor within operating activities.

Lease Disclosures

There are a considerable number of required disclosures for leases. In this section, we provide descriptions of these disclosures for the lessee and the lessor, as well as a few additional disclosures related to sale and leaseback transactions.

Lessee Disclosures

The following disclosure requirements related to leases must be followed by the *lessee* in its financial statements:

Nature of the Leases

- General description of the leases
- The basis upon which variable lease payments are calculated
- The nature of any lease extension or termination options
- The nature of any residual value guarantees
- The nature of any restrictions imposed by leases
- The nature of any leases that have not yet commenced, that will create significant rights and obligations for the lessee
- The significant assumptions and judgments made, including whether a lease exists, the allocation of consideration to leases, and the determination of the lease discount rate

Lease Costs

- The finance lease cost, separately reporting the amortization of right-of-use assets and the interest expense on lease liabilities
- The operating lease cost
- The short-term lease cost, not including leases with a term of one month or less
- The variable lease cost
- The income from subleases
- The net gain or loss on sale and leaseback transactions

Other Information

- Cash paid for items included in the measurement of lease liabilities
- Non-cash information regarding lease liabilities caused by securing right-of-use assets
- The weighted-average remaining lease term
- The weighted-average discount rate
- A maturity analysis of finance lease liabilities and operating lease liabilities, which reveals undiscounted cash flows for each of the first five years and the total for all subsequent years

- A reconciliation of undiscounted cash flows to the finance lease liabilities and operating lease liabilities recognized in the balance sheet
- All lease transactions between related parties
- Disclosure of a policy to account for short-term leases without the recognition of a lease liability or right-of-use asset
- Disclosure of a policy to not separate lease components from non-lease components, and the classes of underlying assets to which it applies

SAMPLE LESSEE DISCLOSURE

(000s)	Year Ending December 31,	
	20X4	20X3
Lease cost		
Finance lease cost:		
Amortization of right-of-use assets	$1,320	$1,295
Interest on lease liabilities	475	463
Operating lease cost	280	240
Short-term lease cost	72	65
Variable lease cost	11	9
Sublease income	40	10
Total lease cost	$2,198	$2,082
Other Information		
(Gains) and losses on sale and leaseback transactions	$--	$400
Cash paid for amounts included in the measurement of lease liabilities		
Operating cash flows from finance leases	810	615
Operating cash flows from operating leases	275	228
Financing cash flows from finance leases	460	420
Weighted-average remaining lease term – finance leases	4.7 years	4.3 years
Weighted-average remaining lease term – operating leases	3.0 years	2.9 years
Weighted-average discount rate – finance leases	6.9%	6.5%
Weighted-average discount rate – operating leases	7.2%	7.0%

Lessor Disclosures

The following disclosure requirements related to leases must be followed by the *lessor* in its financial statements:

Nature of the Leases

- General description of the leases
- The basis upon which variable lease payments are calculated
- The nature of any lease extension or termination options
- The nature of any options for a lessee to purchase an underlying asset
- The existence of any lease transactions between related parties

Significant Judgments Made

- The significant assumptions and judgments made, including whether a lease exists, the allocation of consideration to lease and non-lease components, and the determination of the amount the lessor expects to derive from the underlying asset at the end of the lease term
- How the lessor manages the risk associated with the residual value of its leased assets, including the following:
  - Its risk management strategy for residual assets
  - The carrying amount of the residual assets that are covered by residual value guarantees
  - Other means by which the lessor acts to reduce its residual asset risk

Financial Statement Recognition

- A tabulation of lease income for the annual and interim reporting period, which includes:
  - For sales-type and direct financing leases, the profit or loss recognized at the commencement date, as well as interest income
  - For operating leases, the lease income related to lease payments
  - Lease income related to variable lease payments that were not included in the measurement of the lease receivable
- The components of the aggregate net investment in sales-type and direct financing leases

Additional Disclosures for Sales-Type and Direct Financing Leases

- Explain any significant changes in the balance of the lessor's unguaranteed residual assets, as well as the deferred selling profit on its direct financing leases
- Provide a maturity analysis of the lessor's lease receivables, stating the undiscounted annual cash flows for each of the next five years and the total receivables remaining thereafter.

- Reconcile the undiscounted cash flows to the lease receivables stated in the balance sheet.

Additional Disclosures for Operating Leases

- Provide a maturity analysis of lease payments, stating the undiscounted annual cash flows for each of the next five years and the total amounts remaining thereafter. This analysis is to be stated separately from the analysis for sales-type and direct financing leases.
- Separately make all fixed asset-related disclosures for underlying assets from all other assets that are owned by the lessor.

Practical Expedient Disclosures

If the lessor chose to not separate non-lease components from an associated lease component and account for them as a single component, the following disclosures are required:

- The fact that it chose the practical expedient.
- The classes of assets for which the lessor made the election.
- The nature of the applicable lease and non-lease components that were combined, as well as any non-lease components that were not eligible, and so were not combined.
- The topic (either ASC 606, *Revenue Recognition*, or ASC 842, *Leases*) being applied to the combined component.

Sale and Leaseback Transactions

A seller-lessee in a sale and leaseback transaction should disclose the primary terms and conditions of the transaction. In addition, it should separately disclose any gains or losses from the transaction, so that they are not aggregated into the gains or losses derived from the disposal of other assets.

Summary

The key elements of the accounting for leases by the lessee are as follows:

- An organization must recognize assets and liabilities for the rights and obligations created by leases that have terms of more than 12 months.
- Leases are classified as either finance leases or operating leases, both of which are capitalized by the lessee.
- The lessee can choose not to capitalize a lease with a term of 12 months or less.
- The lease term is the non-cancellable part of the lease agreement, plus any periods for options to extend the lease when it is reasonably certain that the lessee will exercise the option.

- The expense associated with an operating lease is recorded on a straight-line basis and presented as a single line item on the income statement, which combines interest and amortization.
- The interest and amortization expense associated with a finance lease is recorded on an accelerated basis and is presented as two line items on the income statement, where interest expense and amortization expense are separated.

The key elements of the accounting for leases by the lessor are as follows:

- The lessor can recognize a lease as either a sales-type lease, a direct financing lease, or an operating lease.
- The sales-type lease classification is used when the lessee is expected to use a major part of the economic benefits of the asset; this is likely to be the classification used for most non-property assets. For this lease, the lessor derecognizes the asset, recognizes any profit at the lease commencement date, and records a lease receivable and a residual asset, as well as interest income over the course of the lease.
- The direct financing lease classification is used when a lease is not a sales-type lease, the present value of the lease payments is 90% or more of the fair value of the asset, and the lessor will probably collect the lease payments. For this lease, the lessor defers the selling profit and defers recognition of any initial direct costs.
- The operating lease classification is used when a lease does not qualify as either a sales-type or direct financing lease. For this lease, the lessor retains the asset on its balance sheet and recognizes lease income over the term of the lease.

The very high level of disclosure required for leases results in a substantial amount of transparency regarding a lessee's financial leverage and its leasing activities. Unfortunately, it also introduces a greater degree of complexity to the accounting for leases. Consequently, it may be useful to create a procedure for the leasing transactions that an entity engages in most frequently, along with accompanying examples, and rigidly adhere to that procedure when accounting for leases. It may also be useful to structure leasing transactions in the future so that the procedure can be applied to them. Doing so reduces the potential variability in the accounting that may be applied to leasing transactions, which in turn reduces the risk of having errors creep into the financial statements.

Glossary

C

Commencement date. The date on which an asset is made available for use to a lessee by a lessor.

Consideration. Something of value that induces the parties to a contract to exchange mutual performances.

Contract. An agreement between at least two parties, under which each party acquires rights and duties related to the other party.

D

Direct financing lease. A financing arrangement in which the lessor acquires assets and leases them to its customers, with the intent of generating revenue from the resulting interest payments. This designation is used by the lessor.

Discount rate. The rate implicit in a lease; if this rate cannot be determined, the incremental borrowing rate is used instead.

E

Economic life. The period over which an asset is expected to be economically usable.

F

Fair value. The price that would be received to sell an asset or paid to transfer a liability, between market participants in an orderly transaction as of the measurement date.

Finance lease. A leasing arrangement in which ownership of the underlying asset effectively passes to the lessee by the end of the lease. This designation is used by the lessee.

I

Incremental borrowing rate. The rate of interest at which a lessee would have to borrow funds, using collateral and over a period of time that equals a set of lease payments.

Initial direct costs. A cost that is only incurred if a lease agreement occurs.

L

Lease. An arrangement under which a lessor agrees to allow a lessee to control the use of identified property, plant, and equipment for a stated period of time in exchange for one or more payments.

Lease liability. The obligation by a lessee to make payments arising from a lease, as calculated on a discounted basis.

Lease modification. An alteration of the terms and conditions of a contract that triggers a change in the consideration for or scope of a lease.

Lease receivable. The right of a lessor to obtain lease payments from either a sales-type lease or a direct financing lease.

Lease term. The period of a lease that cannot be cancelled, which can include reasonably certain extension options.

Lessee. An entity that obtains the right to use an asset for a defined time period in exchange for consideration.

Lessor. An entity that agrees to provide the right to use an asset for a defined time period in exchange for consideration.

M

Market participants. The buyers and sellers in the principal market for an asset or liability that are independent of each other, are knowledgeable, are able to enter into a transaction, and are willing to do so.

O

Operating lease. Any lease other than a finance lease, from the perspective of the lessee. Any lease other than a sales-type lease or a direct financing lease, from the perspective of the lessor.

Orderly transaction. A transaction that allows sufficient time for usual and customary marketing activities prior to a sale.

P

Penalty. Any requirement for a lessee to pay cash, incur a liability, perform services, or to otherwise suffer an economic detriment.

Period of use. The time period during which an asset is employed to fulfill a contract.

Probable. When a future event is likely to occur.

R

Rate implicit in a lease. The rate of interest that causes the present value of lease payments and the ending asset value to equal the sum of the fair value of an asset, less any investment tax credit and any deferred lessor initial direct costs.

Residual value guarantee. A guarantee made by a lessee to the lessor, that the value of a leased asset will be at least a certain amount at the end of the lease.

Right-of-use asset. A lessee's right to use an asset over the term of a lease.

S

Sales-type lease. A leasing arrangement in which the collectability of minimum lease payments is predictable and there are no important uncertainties about the amount of unreimbursable costs yet to be incurred. This designation is used by the lessor.

Glossary

Selling profit or loss. An amount as of the commencement date that equals the fair value of the underlying asset, minus the carrying amount of the underlying asset net of any unguaranteed residual asset, minus any lessor initial direct costs that are deferred.

Short-term lease. A lease that has a term of 12 months or less as of the commencement date.

Standalone price. The price at which a component of a contract would be purchased separately.

Sublease. A transaction in which the primary lease remains in effect, while the lessee re-leases the underlying asset to a third party.

U

Underlying asset. An asset for which the right of use has been shifted to a lessee as part of a lease.

Unguaranteed residual asset. The amount expected to be derived from an underlying asset after a lease term has been completed, and which is not guaranteed by the lessee or any other party.

Useful life. The period over which an asset is expected to directly or indirectly contribute to the cash flows of a business.

V

Variable lease payments. Payments made by a lessee to a lessor that vary due to changes in facts or circumstances over the lease term.

Index

www.ingramcontent.com/pod-product-compliance
Lightning Source LLC
Chambersburg PA
CBHW080723220326
41520CB00056B/7384